This book belongs to

....

....

....

....

CW00863308

Copyright © John Rebholz 2018.

The right of Mr John Rebholz to be identified as the author of this work has been asserted by him in accordance with the Copyright, Designs and Patents Act 1988.

All rights reserved. This book is sold subject to the condition that no part of this book is to be reproduced, in any shape or form. Or by way of trade, stored in a retrieval system or transmitted in any form or by any means, electronic, mechanical, photocopying, recording, be lent, re-sold, hired out or otherwise circulated in any form of binding or cover other than that in which it is published and without a similar condition, including this condition being imposed on the subsequent purchaser, without prior permission of the copyright holder.

Illustrations by Zoe Saunders.

Printed in Great Britain by Lightning Source.

A CIP catalogue record for this book is available from the British Library.

Paperback ISBN 978-1-9164386-0-6

Hardcover ISBN 978-1-9164386-1-3

We are all just not ordinary...
(A poem for us all)

Every one of us has a story to tell;

Without them, we would not have a tomorrow.

Thanks to them we had a yesterday.

Every spoken word and every single thought

Brings back to life our cherished departed.

Their memories are picture books delivered from Heaven;

We must talk about them, celebrate them and relive them,

For as long as we do they will forever walk by our side.

J Rebholz, March 2018

Rebholz Family Tree 1879 - 2018

Meet the Characters...

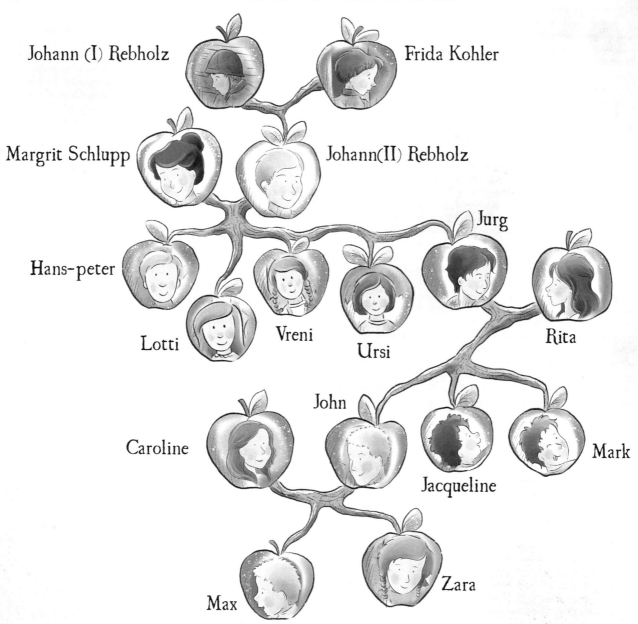

Johann (I) Rebholz · Frida Kohler · Margrit Schlupp · Johann(II) Rebholz · Hans-peter · Lotti · Vreni · Ursi · Jurg · Rita · Caroline · John · Jacqueline · Mark · Max · Zara

The Apple Tree

Story by John Rebholz

Illustrations by Zoe Saunders

We see a father and his son cosy up so tight,
To hear a much loved story, read almost every night.

This happens right across the world, several million times,

As children wait so patiently for those bedtime chimes.

Not any story this one, so he'll recall it well:

A precious tale for children, who will all retell...

Not so far away and not so long ago

Lived a boy and his family we'll get to know.

The family lived on a ramshackle farm,

In a modest cottage, more like a barn!

They lived in a country, so beautiful and bright
Hand-crafted by God, no doubt, this sight:
Tall were the mountains and free were the streams,
With colourful landscapes completing these scenes.

He had three doting sisters and an older brother

Who loved to run and play outside, chasing one another.

Being poor in those days meant play was up to you,
Rollerskates were still great fun; with just one not two!

For they were loved and happy in every single way,

Waiting on their father's return from a long, hard day.

To be together, to eat together with their family as one,

So sealed the fate of happy times: the father and his son.

Their father, Johann, knew only too well,

As we'll hear from the story he had to tell,

That the love of a family is what we all crave,

For he knew not his father, a soldier so brave.*

The years went by and nobody knew

That this poor man had lived and grew

Not knowing his father, which made him so sad,

So he more than most treasured all that he had.

*Johann Rebholz I (22.02.1917, Prussian Corps, Picardy, France)

For back in the dark years of World War One,

Our German soldier guarded more than his gun.

Inside his uniform, sewn tight and secure,

Was a pouch, a note and some seeds to endure.

He'd fought for a lost cause, his hope to return

To the family he loved and for a life he did yearn.

But he knew that through nature he would survive;

With these seeds of life to keep his memory alive.

And the war-torn note – what did that say?

What did it pass on from then to this day?

That the love of a father knows no earthly bounds.

It read:

From the Father
You'll never know…

and so he was found.

His little grandson did all that he could

To please his dad and be understood.

Making him smile meant the world to him,

And planting the tree made them both widely grin.

The tree's seeds were planted as autumn winds blew,

But this story means more than just me and you:

It's a story of life and how we all grow.

Below ground is busy, though nothing yet shows.

Then over time, a small tree did appear,

From the busy times of the previous years.

A reminder of how fast times change and move,

From something so small, yet so great it would prove.

The little boy has grown up fast, a soldier he's become,

To proudly serve his homeland and to please his mum.

Trained for the 'cold war' – or whoever was the foe,

This was my dad, a grenadier, so proud I was to know!

A kind, handsome man, he stood six feet tall,

But leaving his home was so hard for them all.

Now begins his journey as a striking young man,

And dreams of his own home slowly began.

Travelling abroad, he meets a young lady

Who shared his wacky humour and strong sense of duty;

Both were so young, so happy and free,

But they came from different countries, a problem, you see.

The love-spark ignited
meant words were no barrier;
Apart though they were,
their dream made them happier,
For they both knew
they'd be together again,
So this part of the story
began through their pen.

The tall English girl with the grey-blue eyes
Has made an impression through many replies;
They write to each other to and fro,
Love-letters flowing
from peaks topped with snow.

It's summer when father sees son next at home,

Where the seeds they had planted are now fully grown.

The roots grow strong and red apples appear,

Though all things are changing their love stays sincere.

Fate brings the young couple together once more
With thoughts of the world they're about to explore,

Though never forgetting
what they'll leave behind
but sure in the
knowledge the tree's
there to find.

For their greatest
chapter is about to start:

A wedding,
then children who
stole their hearts.

Three new lives that
blossomed like the tree,

And playing in its shadow:
my brother, sister and me.

Please don't be sad or have any fear;

The next stage of the apple tree will bring a tear.

This tree lived its life, and bore many fruits

But now it makes room for brand-new shoots.

Thinking of past times, I remember that tree

As I gaze out of the window; looking back at me

I see a loving father and son snuggled tight,

A happy story being read, for the first time that night.

This story – so precious – he'll recall it well
Of a dad so great and a time so swell.

It's your time to grow up,
but promise me this:
You'll forever tell this story
of a time we all miss,

Then his chapter in our story
will carry on through,

As mine will
from you ...

Dedications

To my beloved dad, you are my everything. All that I am, I owe to you and Mum. I will never forget you. You are in my thoughts every day. "God saves his greatest battles for his bravest soldiers" – this is how I remember you, the bravest soldier that ever lived. Until we meet again, Grossi, this book is dedicated to your life and your memory. This book belongs to you.

I would also like to thank my family for the support, inspiration, and unconditional love through this life-changing time: my loving wife and best friend Caroline, my beautiful daughter Zara 'Zee', and my handsome son Max. You are all my world!

Special thanks to my greater family: to my brother Mark and sister Jax for all the hard times we've endured together and the happier times ahead.
Thank you for being there when I needed you. Semper Fidelis.

A big thank you to the most gifted illustrator, Zoe Saunders, who gave my story 'life'!

I reserve a special thanks to my very talented mum, without whom my dream of completing my first written story would not have been possible.
You mean the world to our family – you are <u>my rock!</u>

I also dedicate this short story to all those who are suffering, or those who have suffered, with the loss of a loved one; today my thoughts are with you.

Be strong and keep their memory alive – talk about them, share stories, read, draw, write songs about them, never forget them and they will live on through you.

My father battled bravely with advanced stage prostate cancer for two years. I also have a debt of gratitude to all the NHS healthcare professionals who treated him after his terminal diagnosis.

The 'pioneering' team at Cambridge Oncometrix gave me hope for the future – through research we will win against this illness.

We would urge readers to support Prostate Cancer charities and Children's mental health organisations.

The Apple Tree (My Dad and Me) is a true short story of a son remembering his father after he passes away from an illness. The tale takes the reader on a journey through three generations of his family, the kind of life his father had, his adventures, and more importantly what he has created, represented in parallels by nature and its 'life-cycle'.

The Apple Tree represents and mirrors his own life, from when he planted the seeds with his own father all those years ago. It is also a reflection of how I turned a story of my dad into a story of how we all live out our 'life-cycle', creating loving memories along the way; memories that we must pass onto the next generation.

As the beautiful tree grows and blossoms, so does the story of the narrator, his father and his own story. Memories are captured as a story to keep his greatly missed and loving father's spirit alive.

This is a message that each family's stories are inevitably entwined in one another's, from the very beginning to the sad conclusion of all that is good on Earth.

For years I struggled to come to terms with my father's illness and his eventual passing. To make sense of my emotions and the many questions, particularly from my children about their Grossi (Swiss for Grandad) becoming sick and dying, I decided to write them a story about life. I couldn't find a children's book that tackled this subject in a way that encapsulated this theme, in-line with something from nature they could relate to (a tree), so I decided to write one myself.

I have never written before, but something genuinely stirred inside me, a parting gift I like to call it from my father. My objectives for writing this story are primarily to keep the memories of loved ones alive, by celebrating their accomplishments, encouraging families and especially young ones to talk about their loss. I also would like to raise awareness about children's mental health and the use of an art-form (such as drawing, painting, music, writing, drama and so on) as a means of expressing and coming to terms with the grief and pain of bereavement.

In memory of my beloved Father:
Jurg 'Grossi' Rebholz: Bettingen (CH)
25.05.1945 – Camberley (GB) 18.08.2016

Lightning Source UK Ltd.
Milton Keynes UK
UKRC010255171118
332422UK00003B/86